FLOWER ARRANGEMENTS
Month by Month · Step by Step

This book is a must for all flower, garden and home lovers, for it covers every facet of the art of Flower Arranging and the growing and buying of flowers for decoration.

Already the author of fifteen best-selling books on the subject Julia Clements, whose name is synonymous with flowers, has created this book to appeal not only to those already practised in the art but to those who may not have the time to read through lots of instruction and explanation of its intricacies.

The book has been arranged by months and the full page colour arrangements are illustrated with step-by-step drawings to help those who wish to make a quick arrangement at any given month of the year. The reader need only turn to the relevant season and follow the instructions of the chosen arrangements. She can then pick or buy similar flowers and create her own picture. To further the interest of the reader, there are hints on what to buy, when to plant, how to do it, preservation of flowers, unusual designs, the modern approach, dry arrangements, and how to make flowers live longer. In fact it is a book no flower lover can be without.

The Royal Horticultural Society awarded Julia Clements, in February 1974, the Victoria Medal of Honour, their highest award.

Julia Clements

FLOWER ARRANGEMENTS

MONTH BY MONTH · STEP BY STEP

B T Batsford Limited   London

First published in 1974 by the
Hutchinson Publishing Group,
whose © line illustrations are
included in this impression by
courtesy of the original publishers.

ISBN 0 7134 4720 6

Printed and bound in Hong Kong
for the publishers
B T Batsford Ltd
4 Fitzhardinge Street
London W1H 0AH

Contents

Introduction

If you enjoy having flowers in the home, then this is the book for you. If you have not already discovered the pleasure of artistically arranging flowers, I can assure you that great delights are in store for you.

Whether you see in flowers the excitement of colour or love them as the result of the grower's skill, whether you find in them all the textures and shapes you need to group into a pleasing decorative pattern or like to gaze on them for spiritual refreshment, they are there, almost everywhere, all the time, for you.

If you have the slightest urge to do something creative, and most of us have at some time or another, you need only buy or pick a few flowers and place them in a container according to a few basic principles: tall and fine at the top or outside, bigger and round down the centre, medium flowers in between. Almost at once, you will see the result in a lovely living picture. It is easy accessibility of the basic material which makes the subject of arranging flowers so simple, yet fascinating. Maybe your reason for wanting to do the flowers is not creative but functional. Guests may be coming to dinner, or you have a bunch which just needs placing somewhere. But how and where, you might ask?

It is the first step which often seems the most difficult. Many feel shy, thinking that others know better. Make no mistake: most do not. They know better what *they* want to do, but you are doing what *you* want to do and feel. Always remember that flower arranging is an expressive art, and if you approach it as such, you will put a little of yourself into every arrangement you make. You will at times, I trust, make a certain design because you feel like it. If so, that will be the true reason for your doing it.

You may one day just want to mass a bunch of yellow daffodils in a pewter mug because the colour yellow makes you feel gay and happy. On another occasion, you will carefully plan a pink and mauve arrangement because these colours remind you of a sentimental happening. Or you may just want to thrust a few flowers into a bowl of fruit. *Everything you do is right for you.* You are the artist and you have every right to say, 'I like them like this'.

Of course there are many facets of flower arranging. Many true gardeners dislike cutting the flowers short in order to make a design, but just as a couturier has to cut into a length of beautiful cloth in order to make a creation, so the flower arranger has to cut her flowers to enable her to make a picture with them. Some flower arrangers wish to compete at shows, and therefore must learn how to follow the strict rulings of the show schedule. Some only wish to have a few in the house, while others like to study the subject in order to be creative.

Thinking of the many books I have written in the past, and of the great advance we have all made in the subject, I became concerned as to whom I should address this new one. I was not sure whether to make it modern, using only a few flowers to suit those who live in town, or whether to suggest mass country arrangements, realising those in town would suffer agonies at not being able to obtain the flowers. I first thought of this book as a help to beginners, but then I wondered if those who had followed me faithfully over the years might think I had taken a retrograde step and was without ideas. Then I remembered my father who once said, 'You cannot please everyone all of the time', and I hope I have varied the book enough to please most of you some of the time.

Since I began in 1947, when I toured the country hoping to bring beauty with flowers into the lives of war-weary women, I have had the good fortune to make a world tour, speaking, teaching and demonstrating flower arranging in many countries, including France, Germany, Italy, Monaco, Pakistan, Belgium, Thailand, Australia, New Zealand, Japan, Canada and the USA. This experience has not only widened my horizons but also made me realise how much more I have to learn.

I have discovered in the course of my travels that if you love flowers – and who does not? – you have friends in every country in the world. I have also learned that there is probably no greater common denominator in the world than flowers, for surely they are loved by all. They are not manufactured by one exclusive country, nor are they one person's particular invention or right. They are Nature's gifts for everyone and are to be found in all sizes, shapes, varieties and colours in virtually every part of the world.

There is not a lot of reading in this book, nor are there many technicalities to absorb. These facets of the subject I have covered in other books that deal with show work. In this book I show by drawings how each flower arrangement is made, so that it can easily be done by anyone, anywhere. If you like the design and cannot obtain the plant material I show, just get something similar in form, shape or size, for it is placing different forms together that helps you create a picture.

Always have an arranger's proper tools at hand: flower scissors, containers, wire netting and Oasis. Whether you live in town or country, grow your flowers or buy them, I trust you will always enjoy them – they will not only bring pleasure to you through arranging them expressively, but also great joy to all who see them.

Julia Clements
Chelsea, London

My thanks are due to Jon Whitbourne for the excellent photography in this book, and also to Nigel Coomber for the finished line drawings, and to Miss Elspeth Napier of the Royal Horticultural Society for checking the manuscript.

Lengthening the Life of Cut Flowers

Nothing is more frustrating than to have spent money, time and skill in arranging flowers for a special event, only to find them drooping a few hours later.

Many methods have been expounded for lengthening the life of cut flowers, each dealing expertly with one particular type of flower. But if we tried to carry out all of this advice, we would spend the best part of the day wondering which flower to put with which and whether we should cut, burn, strip or dip the stem ends in this, that or the other.

So, in order to help, I list below some of the hints that have proved very valuable to me, although the most careful calculations can sometimes be upset by climatic conditions or the time of picking or buying the flowers.

1   Try to pick at night or early morning when transpiration is at its lowest. If buying, always do so the day before flowers are needed.

2   Strip off all lower leaves and recut stems, leaving them in deep water for some hours or overnight to become fully charged with water.

3   All woody-stemmed flowers, such as lilac, chrysanthemum, flowering shrubs and roses, should have their stem ends split and lower leaves removed before placing in deep water.

4   All leaves and leafy twigs should be submerged in a bath of water for hours before using. This makes them turgid and strong.

5   If flowers arrive by post or other means and are wilted, recut the stem ends and place in hot water. This of course does not apply to soft stemmed flowers, but roses revive miraculously with this treatment as do all flowering shrubs.

6   Always have warm water in the container before starting your arrangement; this prevents the stem ends drying out. A tablet of charcoal in the water will keep it pure. Top up with room temperature water each day.

7 Sugar in the water will help most flowers (with the exception of daffodils and narcissi which exude a sticky substance). Use two teaspoonfuls to a pint of water. Today we are lucky to have on the market two excellent cut flower preservatives: Bio Flowerlife and Chrysal powder, both of which I have tried with excellent results.

8 Some flowers, such as dahlias, poppies and euphorbias, exude a milky substance. These will last longer if the cut stems are held under a running hot tap or stood in about two inches of hot water for about 10 seconds. This disperses the substance.

9 Always remove the white portion of the stem ends of many bulbous flowers such as tulips; they can only drink through the green part of the stem.

10 To keep bought tulips from bending over, pierce the stem an inch below the flower head with a pin. Wrap them in paper up to the heads and steep in deep water for some hours or overnight.

Do try experimenting yourself with any items I have not mentioned and get to know your flowers. But remember: 1) always to recut the stem ends before arranging them, 2) split all woody-stemmed flowers at the ends, 3) submerge all leaves in water for some hours before using, 4) always put water in the vase before starting the arrangement, adding whatever preservative you choose and 5) top up with water when needed. If you follow these five instructions I am sure your flower arrangements will give pleasure for many more days than you would expect.

THE MONTHS

Just One

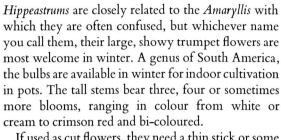

Hippeastrums are closely related to the *Amaryllis* with which they are often confused, but whichever name you call them, their large, showy trumpet flowers are most welcome in winter. A genus of South America, the bulbs are available in winter for indoor cultivation in pots. The tall stems bear three, four or sometimes more blooms, ranging in colour from white or cream to crimson red and bi-coloured.

If used as cut flowers, they need a thin stick or some support inside their hollow, fleshy stems. Here I show one of the four blooms picked from my pot plant which had practically finished blooming. This flower lived for another week.

The container is a Moroccan pottery water bottle. I have since made something similar by using two bottles, covering them with thick plaster filler powder (Polyfilla) to which I added a little brown dye and a few spots of glycerine to prevent cracking.

Step 1—Place the piece of Manzanita wood in a downward position, pressing it on to a lump of plasticine. Any other pieces of root or twisted wood will do equally well.

Step 2—Add two short pieces of pine, one upwards, the other downwards.

Step 3 (opposite)—Add the single flower of *Hippeastrum*. Should you not wish to fill the bottle(s) with water, the flower can be placed in a tube of water inserted in the bottle opening.

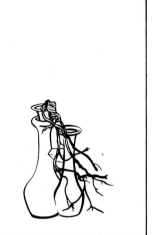

Step 1

Step 2

Choice Shrubs

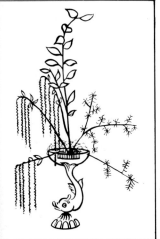

Choice shrubs from the garden are a delight at any time, but are especially welcome in the beginning of the year. There is no need to pick a lot, but provided the bushes are well established, a few stems cut here and there will cause no damage and can create a pleasing picture.

Here a tall spray of that glossy yellow/green edged shrub *Elaeagnus pungens* 'Maculata' is placed with the tassels of *Garrya elliptica* and the starry, strap-like flowers of *Hamamelis mollis* (witch hazel). Placed centrally are the pale green heads of *Viburnum opulus* 'sterile' (guelder rose), while below them is the green *Helleborus corsicus*. The *Skimmia* with reddish flower heads is Waterer's 'Bronze Knight'.

All of these woody-stemmed leaves and flowers should be split at the stem ends and stood in warm water for some hours before arranging.

Step 1 — Place a pinholder in the bottom of the vase with wet Oasis. Oasis can be obtained from the florist. Crumpled wire netting over the pinholder is an alternative. Then insert the tall stem first, followed by the tassels of *Garrya elliptica* on one side and *Hamamelis mollis* on the other.

Step 2 — Add the pale green round head of *Viburnum opulus* 'sterile' down the centre with the *Hellebores* protruding over the rim.

Step 3 (opposite) — Insert the stems of *Skimmia* at both sides and at the back, adding the *Arum italicum* leaves at the base. Fill the vase with water and top up each day.

Step 1

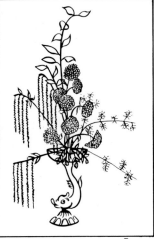

Step 2

A Growing Garden

In addition to flowering bulbs in pots and small clusters of early flowers tucked between moss in shallow containers, January is the time when a growing garden is most welcome.

Here several small pot plants are combined with bark in a vegetable tureen. Should you not want to make the garden yourself, many florists or nurserymen will plant your own container for you. Choose plants of varying form, size and colour. Mine uses various shades of green and white.

Step 1—Place some stones or crocks with crushed charcoal in the base of the dish and cover lightly with soil. Remove the plants from their pots. Insert the tallest plant at the back (mine is Maidenhair fern), then the trailing ones at the sides (e.g. Ivy or *Sedum sieboldii*), and add a piece of bark. Press these in well, adding more soil to keep them in position.

Step 1

Step 2—Next add a *Chlorophytum* (Spider Plant) leaning backwards, and a green and white marble-like *Peperomia* in the front with a white Daisy plant behind it (optional).

Step 3 (opposite)—After adding more soil and watering it, cover the surface with bun moss or that lovely *Helxine* with the tiny, pale green leaves. Pin the moss down to the soil with the aid of hairpins and water it well. Add water daily and spray overhead if possible.

Step 2

Subtle Greens

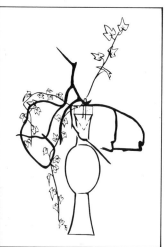

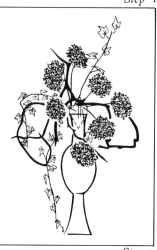

Hydrangeas, picked from the underside of the bush in October or November, are usually of a pale green colouring. Some are blue/green, others pink/green, and if stood in a few inches of water after picking and allowed to dry out in a warm room, they will retain their shape and colour for many months.

I used a dark blue-green pottery container by Phyllis Sherwood to hold these dried, green/blue *hydrangeas* which I picked in late October. The glossy dark green trails of Ivy together with the grey twists of wood give this arrangement an air of muted colours.

Step 1—Place the twists of wood (bare branches are an alternative) into the narrow neck of the container, adding one spray of Ivy flowing downwards and another more upright. If you are not dexterous enough in placing your branches into an open-necked vase by resting them against the inside, try inserting a thick piece of stem crosswise as a cross bar, just below the rim, or insert a small block or wedge of wet Oasis. The wood can then rest under the bar or be held firm on the Oasis by a heavy hairpin or piece of wire.

Step 2—Add the lower swerved *hydrangea* and those which appear more on the exterior of the pattern.

Step 3 (opposite)—Fill in with shorter stems, making sure that some are placed more 'in' than others so that you do not get a flat effect. Add more *hydrangeas* at the back. The Oasis should be kept wet to give life to the Ivy. You could make this design in October in wet Oasis, allowing it to dry out as it is. Sprayed with gold or any other colour at Christmas time, and with a few baubles added, the display would take a festive air.

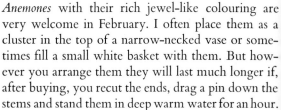

Jewel Bright

Anemones with their rich jewel-like colouring are very welcome in February. I often place them as a cluster in the top of a narrow-necked vase or sometimes fill a small white basket with them. But however you arrange them they will last much longer if, after buying, you recut the ends, drag a pin down the stems and stand them in deep warm water for an hour.

Here, in a tall Clive Brooker pottery container, they are used with *rhododendron* leaves and a twig of hawthorn.

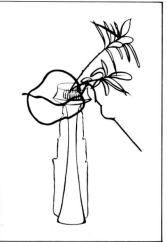

Step 1—Place a pinholder in the top of the vase and lay the twisted piece of Ivy root across the top. According to the shape of the wood you might need a lump of plasticine or a piece of wire to hold it firm. Add two short stems of *rhododendron* swerving out at the right.

Step 1

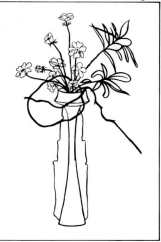

Step 2—Insert the *Anemones* casually with the shorter ones at the base protruding forward.

Step 3 (opposite)—A twig of hawthorn is added for extra effect.

If you have not already done so, now is the time to order seeds of interesting annual flowers. Some of my choices are *Atriplex hortensis* for its lovely red seed panicles, *Amaranthus caudatus* 'Viridis' (green love-lies-bleeding), *Euphorbia marginata* (snow on the mountain) for green and white arrangements, lime green *Nicotiana* (tobacco plant), green *Zinnia* 'Envy', *Nigella* (love-in-a-mist), poppies for seed heads and *Calendula*, 'Apricot Beauty'.

Step 2

Two of a Kind

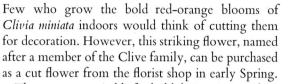

Few who grow the bold red-orange blooms of *Clivia miniata* indoors would think of cutting them for decoration. However, this striking flower, named after a member of the Clive family, can be purchased as a cut flower from the florist shop in early Spring.

They are most suitable for bold designs in a modern setting, although I have seen an effective table centre decoration made with one head of this bloom cut short and placed in a shallow dish surrounded by lemons.

Here I have used two stems, with two sprays of *Viburnum tinus* and driftwood grouped in a Phyllis Sherwood pottery jar.

Step 1—Fill the vase with sand or crumpled newspaper to the base of the neck, then add wet Oasis if you feel this support is needed. Place the branches of weathered wood across the neck of the vase, pinning them down in the Oasis with a hairpin bend of heavy wire to hold them firm. Alternatively press on to plasticine.

Step 2—Insert two sprays of *Viburnum tinus*, one flowering downwards, the other up.

Step 3 (opposite)—Add the *Clivia*, one upright, the other shorter and closer to the rim.

Make sure the stems are constantly in water, for *Clivias* can last up to nine or ten days.

Choisya ternata, *Aucuba*, *Skimmia* and laurel are other evergreen shrubs that can be used at this time of the year, and the design can be copied using any seasonal flowers.

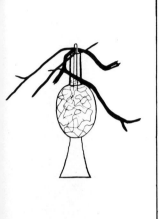

Step 1

Step 2

Oriental Touch

The *Camellia*, named after Camellus, the Moravian Jesuit priest and botanist, is among our most favoured evergreen shrubs. Formerly thought to be tender, since it was often grown in conservatories, it is now known to be perfectly hardy, though it prefers a shady spot.

The handsome glossy foliage is much sought after by flower arrangers for use as a background for large groups, and its various types of flowers are ideal for either table decorations (on short stems), or as the main interest in modern designs.

Here I have used the variety 'Elegans' with a spray of forced *Amelanchier canadensis* blossom.

Step I

Step 1—Place a pinholder in the base of the pottery container and insert two stems of *Camellia* spreading out low at the right, the shorter one pointing more forward.

Step 2—Add two stems of *Amelanchier*, one upright, the shorter one forward.

Step 3 (opposite)—Insert a third *Camellia* upright, further 'in', the forward and backward placements giving a third dimension to the whole.

The ends of all woody-stemmed plants, such as these two, should be split, not only for easier insertion on the pinholder, but also for greater intake of water. Pick *Camellias* in bud, and use warm water with a teaspoonful of sugar.

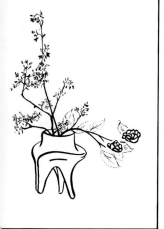

Step 2

Contemporary

Step I

Step 2

Hamamelis mollis (witch hazel), whose starry, strap-like flowers with their lovely scent appear in December through to February, is ideal when placed with the early daffodils we can buy in bud in the shops.

This shrub, which came from China, will give splashes of yellow in the garden, and a few carefully cut twigs will add to the beauty of many indoor decorations during the winter.

Here you see it used in a modern arrangement with yellow daffodils.

Step I—Place a large pinholder at the right of a shallow pottery bowl and insert three sprays – one upright, one leaning out to the right, and another forward and up to the left. The tallest stem should be nearly twice the width of the dish.

Step 2—Add the daffodils starting with the buds, placing each one below the other, some facing forward and some sideways as though growing.

Step 3 (opposite)—Place a large leaf at the back on the right side of the dish, add water and stand a piece of driftwood in front of the holder to cover it. Some trails of Ivy add to the effect.

If you have not already done so, order your flower seeds now, for the choice ones go quickly.

Modern Touch

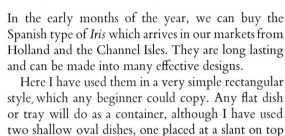

In the early months of the year, we can buy the Spanish type of *Iris* which arrives in our markets from Holland and the Channel Isles. They are long lasting and can be made into many effective designs.

Here I have used them in a very simple rectangular style, which any beginner could copy. Any flat dish or tray will do as a container, although I have used two shallow oval dishes, one placed at a slant on top of the other, for extra effect.

Step 1—Place a large pinholder at the right-hand side of the container. Insert the tallest *Iris*, followed by a shorter one slanting out at the right and another low at the left, to establish height and width. The height of the tallest stem should be one and a half times that of the width of the two containers, but if your *Irises* are not tall enough you can always add a twig or a twisty branch.

Step 2—Add more *Iris* below the tallest stem, each cut shorter than the other.

Step 3 (opposite)—Cut the remaining *Irises* short and add these working in towards the centre. Unify the stems by placing *Arum italicum* leaves towards the base and cover the holder with pebbles, adding a few in the lower dish for extra effect. The bleached Ivy twig is added to give extra height.

Step 1

Step 2

A Drift of Daffodils

Few realise that there are more than 10,000 varieties in the International Register of daffodil names. Many are rare, but for the enthusiast, the choice can still be made from the 500 varieties which are commercially cultivated.

Botanically listed as *Narcissus*, these gay spring flowers are also known as Chalice flowers and Lent lilies. Great poets and writers have sung their praises over the centuries, and the *Narcissus* features in Greek mythology.

Here, however, we are concerned with their practical use, so I show a drift of daffodils designed on a wooden base, heightened by sprays of hazel catkins.

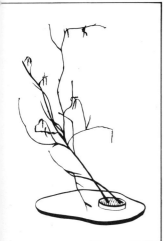

Step 1—Place a tin or dish containing water and a large pinholder at the *right* of the base. Insert the main branch of catkins so that it runs across the base and upwards. Add another twig lower and pointing forward.

Step 1

Step 2—Add the daffodils, each cut shorter than the other, at a slant, and cover the tin of water with a piece of root wood.

Step 3 (opposite)—Place Ivy on the holder at the left back and lower right, finishing with primroses and blue *Muscari* (grape hyacinths). These short flowers can be inserted among the Ivy and moss in small bottles of water.

Step 2

Spring Party

Step 1

Sprays of *Amelanchier canadensis* blossom form the background of this pink, white and cerise spring party group.

This delicate white blossom is sometimes called the 'Snowy Mespilus'. The flowers are certainly snowy in effect during April, yet the red and yellow colouring of the leaves in Autumn is also attractive.

Step 1—Place a pinholder in the base of the container, then fill up with crumpled wire netting allowing it to reach *above* the rim. Add water; then make a triangular pattern with the blossom and white Thalia daffodils. The central stem should be one and a half times taller than the height of vase.

Step 2—Strengthen the centre by inserting pink hyacinths and cerise coloured *Camellias*.

Step 2

Step 3 (opposite)—Fill in by working from outside to centre and from top to bottom with pink double tulips, allowing the low ones to protrude forward over the rim. The stems of the hyacinths and daffodils should be lightly squeezed under a warm running tap to wash away the sticky substance they exude, and then left in deep tepid water for some hours or overnight before arranging them.

Some prefer to use wet Oasis instead of crumpled wire netting to hold the flowers in place, but I find early spring flowers, such as daffodils, tulips and hyacinths, prefer clear water.

Yellow Gay

The choice of a vase is often as important as the flowers that are to go in it. Here a turquoise blue opaque glass vase from Casa Pupo seems ideal for the early yellow double tulips and *freesias* bought from the florist.

Step 1—Fill the vase, or at least the top part, with crumpled wire netting (two-inch mesh), and insert the fine spray of *Amelanchier* blossom in an off-centre pattern, followed by yellow double *freesias*. Have water in the vase before starting to fill up.

Step 2—Place some tulips down the centre making sure that no two heads stand level with each other, and that the one near the rim is placed 'in', the one over the rim 'out'.

Step 3 (opposite)—Add more tulips from outside to inside, with a few flowing backwards to avoid a flat effect.

All winter flowering heathers are effective at this time of the year when placed in a low bowl into which a few *Anemones* or other small flowers are inserted. Indoors, or in the greenhouse, sow some seeds of half hardy annuals, such as *Cobaea scandens*, *Molucella laevis* (bells of Ireland), *Amaranthus caudatus*, (love-lies-bleeding) and Ornamental Strawberry corn. Plant these outside later.

Step 1

Step 2

A Basket Full

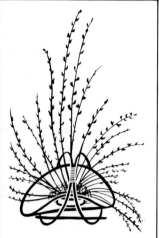

Step 1

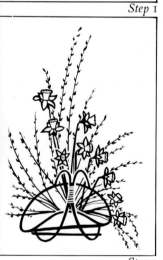

Step 2

While daffodils abound in shops and gardens during the early months of the year the problem is often what leaves to put with them in decoration. Not many leafy twigs last well when cut at this time of the year unless soaked overnight in deep water to which a little sugar has been added (one knob to a pint). However, flowering broom (*Cytisus*) is also in full blossom and swerving sprays of this useful shrub are ideal partners for daffodils and *Narcissi*.

Here the cream *Cytisus praecox* is used as a background for the basket of flowers.

Step 1—Place a bowl in the base of the basket and fill it with a pinholder and wire netting. Make a curved irregular outline with the broom.

Step 2—Start inserting the daffodils in a diagonal line from upper left to lower right.

Step 3 (opposite)—Fill in with shorter blooms and tuck in Ivy leaves around the centre and at the back.

Now is the time to plant corms of *gladioli*. Don't forget the butterfly and *primulinus* varieties which are smaller and easier to handle for decoration. Also sow the seeds of gourds and everlasting flowers such as *Helichrysum Helipterum*, *Statice*, *Xeranthemum* and ornamental grasses. You will need all of these later for autumn and winter arrangements.

Beginner's Piece

This beginner's arrangement is made in a bulbous, narrow-necked Whitefriars glass vase.

There are three steps in this design and three types of plant material are used – tall, flat and dominant. If the flowers are all of the same type, the three steps can be translated by using tall, medium and short, cutting the flowers down to these levels. Alternatively, you can use any plant material, for any design, in the order of points (outside), rounds (centre), and fillers (in between).

Step 1—Insert a tied bunch of any tall leaves or grasses twice the height of the vase. These should stand on the base of the vase or be held by hand until the other items are inserted. No holder is required.

Step 2—Add three *Hosta crispula* leaves. In all its varieties, this plant is invaluable to a flower arranger for its wonderful leaves. *Hostas* can be planted from autumn to spring where you want them to grow permanently. They hate being disturbed.

Step 3 (opposite)—Add some twisted stems of red/ orange azalea. Picked in bud, these flowering shrubs last well in water, especially if the stem ends are split or crushed.

If you have a garden or cool frame, sow seed of the decorative Kale (so useful for winter decorations) and try the climber *Cobaea scandens* for its decorative mauve/green bell flowers. *Phytolacca* (Ink plant or poke weed) is another unusual plant for keen flower arrangers. Sow seed or obtain plants now.

Step 1

Step 2

Double Beauty

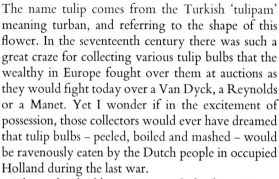

The name tulip comes from the Turkish 'tulipam' meaning turban, and referring to the shape of this flower. In the seventeenth century there was such a great craze for collecting various tulip bulbs that the wealthy in Europe fought over them at auctions as they would fight today over a Van Dyck, a Reynolds or a Manet. Yet I wonder if in the excitement of possession, those collectors would ever have dreamed that tulip bulbs – peeled, boiled and mashed – would be ravenously eaten by the Dutch people in occupied Holland during the last war.

The early double varieties and the later *Paeony* flowering types are my favourites for decoration, leaving the straight soldier-like Darwin tulips in the garden. Planted from mid-September to mid-December, they flower in early spring, although the early doubles can be purchased from the florist from late February onwards.

Step 1

Step 1—Place a pinholder in the base of a container (mine is from Casa Pupo) and fill it with crumpled wire netting or a block of water-soaked Oasis. The pinholder under the Oasis will keep it from toppling over. Start by inserting the longest stems in a low fan shape.

Step 2—Strengthen the centre by adding shorter stems, one below the other, to the rim, the last one protruding forward.

Step 3 (opposite)—Fill in from the outside to the centre, tilting some backwards and adding a few leaves to unify the stems at the lower back. Add water daily.

Step 2

Mixed Creams

Step 1

Step 2

Many town people rely upon the florist for decorative material at this time of the year, and in addition to spring flowers there is an abundant supply of interesting exotic flowers available, such as *Anthuriums*, *Fritillaria* (crown imperial) and *Strelitzia reginae*.

This dainty group combines the cream 'Thalia' narcissi and primrose-coloured *freesias* with some sprigs added from the garden, though snippets from house plants are helpful to those without gardens.

Step 1—Fill the vase with crumpled wire netting and insert the tallest flowers to make an irregular outline.

Step 2—Add shorter flowers down the centre, the lower one protruding forward.

Step 3 (opposite)—Fill in with all stems aimed at the centre. Add some greenery to give depth and some Ivy trails to soften the effect.

If you have a garden, many evergreen shrubs can provide 'tuck-in' leaves for early spring leafless flowers. Shrubs such as *Viburnum tinus*, *Aucuba* (Spotted Laurel), *Rhododendron*, *Ruta graveolens* (Jackman's Blue Rue), *Choisya ternata* (Mexican orange) *Mahonia aquifolium*, and *Fatsia japonica* are among those which no flower arranger should be without for winter and early spring use.

From the Garden

All kinds of blossom and flowers abound in the garden in May. Here you see a mass of *Aquilegias* (columbine), lilac, *Euphorbias*, *Iris*, *Polygonum* (knotweed), honeysuckle, *Spiraea*, *Pulsatilla* seed heads, double *Narcissi* and *Ranunculus*, all casually placed in a Dresden China vase. The flowers should be recut and steeped in deep water for some hours, or overnight, before arranging. This treatment will fully charge the stems with water and so help them last longer.

If you are an Oasis fan, then use it to hold the flowers in place. If you prefer your flowers to stand in clear water, then use a pinholder in the base of the vase and cover this with crumpled wire netting.

Step 1—Fill the vase with the pinholder and wire netting, making sure the wire comes an inch or two above the rim. Tie it down if you think it might move about. Place a few thin flowers to form the shape. Only the central ones need go on to the pinholder.

Step 2—Add shorter flowers down the centre, grouping the colours to your liking.

Step 3 (opposite)—Fill in with more flowers all aimed at the centre, making sure that no two flowers stand level with each other. Place some 'in' and some 'out' to avoid a flat effect, and allow the low front ones to tumble over the rim of the vase. Add water daily.

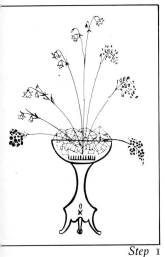

Step 1

Step 2

Ladders to Heaven

Few of us can resist having lilies of the valley in the house during May. Listed in catalogues as *Convallaria* which comes from 'convallis' or valley, the natural habitat of this plant, it is also known in many country areas as 'Ladders to Heaven'.

I love to see them bunched in masses in a basket, but this extravagant use depends upon whether you buy them or pick them from your own garden. I have also made a tall cone of them, using a tall, narrow vase standing inside another wider one. But however you arrange them, their sweet scent will surely delight.

Here I have used a cut glass bonbon jar, combining lilies of the valley with pink Carol roses and a few primulas, which I could not resist.

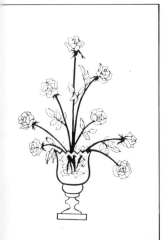

Step 1

Step 1—Fill the vase with crumpled wire netting or a block of wet Oasis, whichever you prefer or have on hand, and make an off-centre outline with some of the roses.

Step 2—Insert the lilies of the valley in between the roses, placing some behind and some protruding forward.

Step 3 (opposite)—Add two shorter roses near the centre and the primulas (optional) wherever you think there is space. Fill up with leaves here and there.

Lilies of the valley should be planted in October or November, but seeds of annual flowers can be sown outside now if the soil has warmed up.

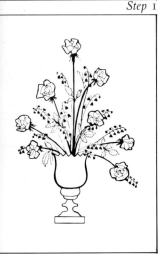

Step 2

Simplicity

Clear water will suffice in the vase for *Rhododendrons* and *Azaleas*, once cut. There is no need to pick a lot, unless of course you need a mass for a party or large hall arrangement. Here is a very simple design using one spray of the variety 'Purple Splendour' which is a small compact-headed flower lasting ten days or more in the house.

Use a tall vase. If you want to make your own, fix two tall round biscuit tins together with a cement or Bostik. Add a shallower tin at the top. Then paint the whole in the colour of your choice. If you prefer a rough surface, add some sawdust to your paint.

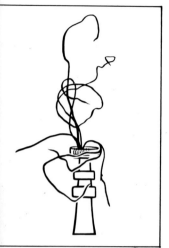

Step 1

Step 1—Place a large pinholder at the left in the base of the cup-shaped top of the container. Insert the tall bleached Ivy twists – one upwards, the other resting on the rim, spreading downwards. Any twigs can be substituted.

Step 2—Add a long curved spray of *Rhododendron*, or two short ones, spreading well out to the right.

Step 3 (opposite)—Insert four *Hosta* leaves, facing each other as though growing. Fill the vase with water and pebbles.

The plant *Hosta*, which commemorates Nicolaus Thomas Host, Austrian botanist of the late eighteenth century, really belongs to the Lily family. Hence its other name, Plantain Lily. Plant it in Autumn or Spring.

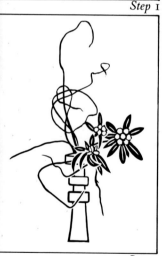

Step 2

Rhythm

Rhythm to some may seem a strange term to apply to flower arrangement, yet movement – the placement of plant material in such a way that the eye flows from the top right down to the rim of the vase, which is emphasised, and then on again to the finish – is termed rhythm.

Here this movement is seen in a modern design using red 'Aladdin' tulips, green broom and pale green *Helleborus corsicus*. Many can manage these designs without using Oasis, but to those who cannot, fix a wedge of wet Oasis in the neck of the vase, allowing it to protrude about an inch above the rim. Fill vase with water.

To get the stems of broom to swerve, bend them under very warm water or wrap them round with newspaper and wire, curving them to the required shape, and leave them in water over night. The tulips also should be stood in deep water over night to strengthen their stems. Draw a pin down the stems of Hellebores and stand them in deep water before being used. This makes the stems stand more firm.

Step 1—Insert a tall swerved stem of broom, allowing it to rise nearly twice the height of the container. Then insert another shorter stem flowing downwards. This stem could be laid across the Oasis and held down by a hairpin.

Step 2—Cut the tulips to different lengths and insert three, one below the other, following the line of the upright piece of broom. Place three more tulips cross wise from right to left.

Step 3 (opposite)—Add short stems of apple-green *Helleborus corsicus* in between the flower stems back and front. Add water daily.

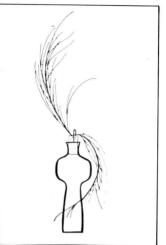

Step 1

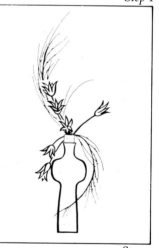

Step 2

Buffet Table

Step 1

Step 2

Open windows, newly mown grass, early flowers often inspire us to bring the garden indoors for summer parties. Even if you live in town, many delightful small flowers can be purchased to make individual table or candelabra decorations.

These pink and white roses were bought from the florist and mixed with Ivy and *Alchemilla*, although carnations, *Freesias*, lilies of the valley, *Stephanotis*, or any other small flowers can be used equally well.

You will need a pair of candle cups to make this arrangement. These can be bought from the florist. Or as an alternative you can place a round block of wet Oasis on a pinholder and stand this in a tin or small saucer placed on top of the candlestick. Fix them with Bostik glue to make them stand firm.

Step 1—Place a candle cup in each of the candlesticks, holding it firm with plasticine, Oasis stick or Bostik. Then add the candle surrounded by some wet Oasis.

Step 2—Insert a short rose near the candle. Then make the low swerving width with a long white rose and sprays of *Alchemilla*, or any fern such as maidenhair, *Asparagus Sprengeri*, with its fern-like trails, or Ivy.

Step 3 (opposite)—Fill in with shorter roses pressed into the Oasis, together with some pinks, making sure some flow forward and others backward to avoid a flat effect.

Some prefer to add wire netting to the candle cups. If you do this, hold it down with a rubber band to prevent it from rising up when the flowers are inserted.

Early Summer

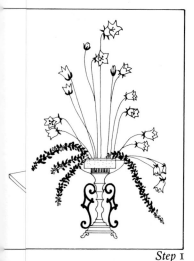

Step I

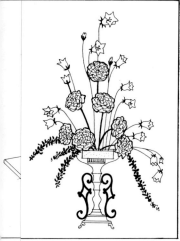

Step 2

The *Paeony* commemorates the ancient Greek physician, Paeon, who claimed to have used *Paeonia officinalis* medicinally. Today it is one of the noblest border plants. It gives those who love cut flowers an infinite variety of blooms in many colours, as well as attractive leaves which continue to supply us with greenery all through the summer until they turn a bronzy colour in the autumn. *Escallonia* is a glossy-leaved shrub which gives pale pink or rose-coloured flowers from June to August, and is often seen in seaside gardens or growing against a wall. Its long swerving sprays make it ideal for the framework of large pedestal groups, or shorter sprays can be used as illustrated here. *Paeonies, Campanulas* and *Escallonia* should have their stems recut and should be stood in deep water before arranging.

Step I—Place a block of wet Oasis on a pinholder and stand this in the base of the container. Crumpled wire netting in the container can be used as an alternative. Make the triangular outline of the design with tall stems of white *Campanula persicifolia* and downward swerving sprays of *Escallonia*.

Step 2—Insert the *Paeonies* so that they occupy the centre of the vase. Some will have to be cut shorter, and you will notice some are placed backwards and others more forward.

Step 3 (opposite)—Fill in with blue annual corn-flowers or any other small flowers and lighten the effect with sprays of pale green *Alchemilla Mollis* (Lady's mantle). Other flowers can be substituted, but notice that the tall thin flowers should be on the outside, the bigger flowers in the centre and medium sized ones used as fillers.

Set Piece

Flower arranging today takes many forms. Instead of the accepted vase of flowers, many find self-expression by creating a picture or a decorative piece. Here, a few heads of the tall 'Queen Elizabeth' rose are placed on a holder and set between two china Casa Pupo doves. For an engagement supper party, I made three of these decorations for the table, without the black base, repeating the theme on a tall stand for the snack bar. Ideal for a low table or sideboard, the decoration is easy to make. The roses are best picked in full bud. After splitting the stem ends the roses will last longer if they stand for an hour or two in deep water with a teaspoonful of sugar added.

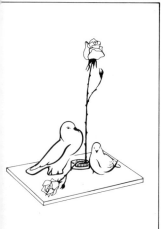

Step I

Step I—I used a large black painted base, although any tray or base will do equally well. Place a well pinholder or a tin containing a pinholder and water in the centre of the tray, standing one dove at the right and the other at the left. Insert the tallest roses for height, adding another long stem rose spreading forward along the base.

Step 2—Add some sprays of the lovely shrub *Stephanandra tanakae* and start filling in with shorter roses.

Step 3—Tuck in shorter roses between the doves, adding short ones at the back so that the decoration can be seen from all sides.

Step 2

Stephanandra is a beautiful shrub related to the *Spiraeas*, giving sprays of pale green leaves tinged with bronze which I have found take well to the glycerine and water method of preservation: see October. The leaves assume a tan colour.

Early Summer

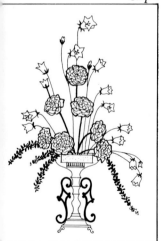

Step 1

The *Paeony* commemorates the ancient Greek physician, Paeon, who claimed to have used *Paeonia officinalis* medicinally. Today it is one of the noblest border plants. It gives those who love cut flowers an infinite variety of blooms in many colours, as well as attractive leaves which continue to supply us with greenery all through the summer until they turn a bronzy colour in the autumn. *Escallonia* is a glossy-leaved shrub which gives pale pink or rose-coloured flowers from June to August, and is often seen in seaside gardens or growing against a wall. Its long swerving sprays make it ideal for the framework of large pedestal groups, or shorter sprays can be used as illustrated here. *Paeonies*, *Campanulas* and *Escallonia* should have their stems recut and should be stood in deep water before arranging.

Step 1—Place a block of wet Oasis on a pinholder and stand this in the base of the container. Crumpled wire netting in the container can be used as an alternative. Make the triangular outline of the design with tall stems of white *Campanula persicifolia* and downward swerving sprays of *Escallonia*.

Step 2—Insert the *Paeonies* so that they occupy the centre of the vase. Some will have to be cut shorter, and you will notice some are placed backwards and others more forward.

Step 2

Step 3 (opposite)—Fill in with blue annual corn-flowers or any other small flowers and lighten the effect with sprays of pale green *Alchemilla Mollis* (Lady's mantle). Other flowers can be substituted, but notice that the tall thin flowers should be on the outside, the bigger flowers in the centre and medium sized ones used as fillers.

Beautiful Leaves

There is an endless variety of forms, shapes and sizes of leaves. In addition their colours are numerous, so open your eyes to the tremendous possibilities of making attractive decorations with leaves only. Here you see a simple home design made with light green *Montbretia* leaves for height, grey *Onopordum* thistle leaves for width, and stems of grey *Stachys lanata* (lamb's tongue) protruding from the centre. Yellow/green fern is also used in the background, and maroon-coloured *Cotinus* (smoke bush) is placed flowing down towards the lower right. Yellow/green Ivy trails are also added at the lower front as well as *Alchemilla mollis* and pale green *Hosta* leaves. All leaves with the exception of the woolly-surfaced type such as lamb's tongue, should be *submerged* in water for some hours to strengthen them. I often add sugar to the water (1 teaspoonful to a pint).

Step 1

Step 1—Fill a shallow dish (or a painted baking tin) with crumpled wire netting placed over a pinholder. Insert the tall leaves through the wire on to the pinholder, followed by the ferns and side grey leaves.

Step 2—Place the maroon-coloured *Rhus* leaves upright at the left and flowing down at the right, followed by stems of the grey *Stachys lanata* slightly pointing forward.

Step 3 (opposite)—Fill in with a burst of striped *Chlorophytum* leaves in the centre and stems of lime green *Alchemilla*, and finish with large *Hosta* leaves at the back and over the front rim with ivy trailing downwards.

Step 2

Such an arrangement can be as colourful as a mixed arrangement of flowers.

Golden Beauty

Nothing is more effective than a mass of roses, and if the roses are scented there is added attraction. These beautifully scented roses, called 'Vanda Beauty', were named by Gregorys after the Vanda Beauty products.

Pick your roses late at night or early morning when transpiration is at its lowest. Pick some in bud and some more open, but leave the fully opened ones on the bush to fade there. Take off all the lower leaves, scrape off the thorns with a sharp knife and split the stem ends, leaving them in deep water for some hours (preferably overnight) before arranging them.

This rose is an early bloomer, and although in full glory in July, I actually photographed these on the second blooming in late September.

Step 1—Place a pinholder in the base of the vase and press on to it a block of wet Oasis. Use crumpled wire netting if you prefer. Make a slightly irregular outline with the tallest roses (the height can be one and a half that of the vase) inserting some low at the sides for width.

Step 2—Add some fine foliage or twigs – I use *Stephanandra* – at the back and insert some of the more fully opened roses in the centre with the lower ones protruding forward over the rim.

Step 3 (opposite)—Fill in with the rest of the roses, adding shorter ones 'inside' and others forward, yet aiming all stems to a point underneath the tallest stem. As a final touch add some striped *Chlorophytum* leaves, or any other leaves with a distinctive note, to break up the uniform gold of the roses.

Roses should be planted in autumn or spring. Order them early.

Step 1

Step 2

Pink and White

Campanulas and *Paeonies* are in the shops and gardens at the same time, and they are easy to combine. The first make good *framework* material, while the second need the *centre* of the stage.

There are as many varieties of *Campanulas* to choose from as there are *Paeonies*, but here I use *Campanula persicifolia* which is a tall, thin, single-bell flowering type, so useful for summer party decorations and church arrangements. Remember, the stems of all flowers should be recut, if possible under water, and stood in deep water for some hours or overnight.

Step 1—Fill the vase with a block of wet Oasis pressed on to a pinholder and insert the stems of campanulas in a tall triangular pattern. The tallest stem should be at least one and a half times higher than the height of the vase. Place the lower side stems almost horizontally into the Oasis.

Step 1

Step 2—Add pink and white *Paeonies* down the centre, cutting some stems shorter than others. Insert the lower ones so that they appear to protrude over the rim.

Step 3 (opposite)—Finally, add two more *Paeonies* low and out at the sides and fill in here and there with stems of the fragile looking lime green *Alchemilla* (Lady's mantle). I love Lady's mantle and have to restrict myself from using it in almost all my summer arrangements. No flower arranger should be without it. Plant it in Autumn or Spring.

Step 2

Garden Pedestal

Lucky are those who can pick from the garden and then run out for extra material if not enough has been gathered. Yet it need not be difficult for those in town if it is remembered that you need about nine tall stems for the outline of a large group, about twelve more important or rounder flowers for the centre, some greenery for the background and two bunches of intermediary flowers for filling in. This is just a general guide, and of course it can be varied.

All the flowers in this group stood in deep water overnight to give them their fill, although the *Paeonies* failed to open fully. I have since discovered that a spoonful of detergent in the water will hasten the opening of tightly budded flowers.

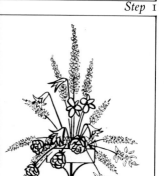

Step 1—Place a large pinholder in the base of the container top of this Rowhurst Forge pedestal and press on to it a block of wet Oasis. The Oasis should rise above the rim of the vase, and since heavy flowers are used, I would advise placing a layer of wire netting over the Oasis. This should be tied down to the container, and it will keep the stems from falling should the Oasis break with the weight of the flowers. It seldom does. Insert the tall *Delphiniums* for height, and lupins and swerving *Weigela* for width.

Step 2—Insert the lilies and *Paeonies*, each cut shorter than the other with some tilting forward.

Step 3 (opposite)—Add blue *Iris* or other flowers around the centre, inserting trailing sprays down the front with leaves at the back. I have also added two stems of green *Euphorbia Wulfenii*. I could not resist them.

Step 1

Step 2

White and Gold

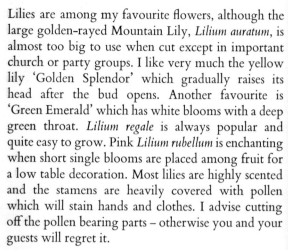

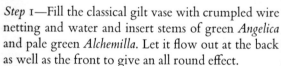

Lilies are among my favourite flowers, although the large golden-rayed Mountain Lily, *Lilium auratum*, is almost too big to use when cut except in important church or party groups. I like very much the yellow lily 'Golden Splendor' which gradually raises its head after the bud opens. Another favourite is 'Green Emerald' which has white blooms with a deep green throat. *Lilium regale* is always popular and quite easy to grow. Pink *Lilium rubellum* is enchanting when short single blooms are placed among fruit for a low table decoration. Most lilies are highly scented and the stamens are heavily covered with pollen which will stain hands and clothes. I advise cutting off the pollen bearing parts – otherwise you and your guests will regret it.

Step 1—Fill the classical gilt vase with crumpled wire netting and water and insert stems of green *Angelica* and pale green *Alchemilla*. Let it flow out at the back as well as the front to give an all round effect.

Step 2—Insert stems of the *regale* lily (pollen removed), some pointing forward, others backwards (unseen), adding a few leaves deep inside near the wire.

Step 3 (opposite)—Insert sprays of white *Philadelphus* blossom here and there allowing this to flow at will.

Now is the time to order some bulbs for flowering in bowls at Christmas time. Ask for the pre-cooled ones that are specially prepared for early flowering.

Step 2

St Paul's Cathedral

Flower decorations in churches can take many forms, for they are created for different reasons. In the photograph is a decoration I made for the American Chapel in St Paul's Cathedral for the Festival of Flowers organised by the National Association of Flower Arrangement Societies.

Made in gold and brown to match the gilded brown woodwork, the asymmetrical outline, placed in the beautiful gilt Lutyens container, is formed with branches of lime flowers and Gold *Eremurus* (Foxtail lilies) backed with brown glycerine-preserved *Magnolia* and Beech leaves, (see August – Country Scene). The centre is emphasised by gold coloured lilies and gilded dry *Alliums*. Gilded skeletonised *Magnolia* leaves complete the effect. This urn was complemented by a similar urn on the other side of the altar against a twenty-two foot high commemorative window, featuring the insignias of the fifty States of the USA.

Step 1—If your vase has a narrow opening, place a deep tin on top of it, fill it to just above the rim with wet Oasis over a large pinholder and cover with wire netting. The asymmetrical outline is made with stripped lime and *Eremurus*. Wild parsley is added for extra height.

Step 2—The lilies are inserted at different levels, some protruding forward, with pale gold carnations placed low at the right to accentuate the swerve.

Step 3 (opposite)—Brown glycerined Beech and *Magnolia* leaves are inserted here and there, with dry *Alliums* sprayed with gold paint. Similarly treated, skeletonised *Magnolia* leaves are added to lighten the effect.

Step 1

Step 2

Country Scene

It is not necessary to be party to a shoot in order to make a decoration with pheasant feathers: by using fruit, vegetables, ferns and feathers, you can make a lovely design suitable for any country home.

You will need two pewter tankards, two large pewter dishes, lemons, artichokes, garlic, ferns and purple *Campanula glomerata*. I love these eighteen inch tall flowers for their heady concentration of colour, but because of their stiff stems I do not enjoy using them except for spots in a design where I need a colour recess. It is a hardy perennial, easy to grow, and is also suitable for a wild garden.

Step 1—Place a tankard on the bottom plate at the right with another plate on top of it. Add a further tankard for height.

Step 2—Behind the top tankard stand a narrow dish containing wet Oasis and insert the ferns, pheasant feathers and purple *Campanulas*. Surround the tankard back and front with lemons and purple-streaked garlic (optional).

Step 3 (opposite)—Add more Oasis to the bottom plate which holds the lower purple flowers and finish with artichokes and lemon. Cover the Oasis with leaves at the back and add purple candles for extra effect.

Now is the time to pick border flowers for drying, such as *Achillea*, *Echinops* (Globe thistle), *Eryngium*, *Lunaria* (honesty), *Helichrysum* and other everlastings. Remove the lower leaves and hang the flowers in small bunches upside down in a dry airy place. Look out also for seed heads, and don't forget to place some sprays of Beech leaves in a solution of one part glycerine and two parts hot water. Leave them for two weeks or more. Although this will turn the leaves brown, they will be pliable and preserved for ever.

Step 1

Step 2

Summer Annuals

Annual flowers and grasses grown from seed sown in March or April should now be blooming in the garden. Here you see a dainty group of grasses, with annual scabious (pincushion flowers), *Asters* and the satiny daisy-like flowers which are listed in the catalogue as *Dimorphotheca*. They are commonly called African daisies because they like the sun.

All of these flowers can be dried for winter decorations. Just place the round blooms on a layer of powdered borax in the bottom of a box and, with a spoon, gently cover the flowers, lifting a petal now and again to avoid a flat effect. Silica gel is another fine powder preparation used for drying flowers. It takes about three weeks for the moisture to be absorbed by the borax method; only three days with the silica gel. Both are obtainable from the chemist. The centre grass (hare's tail grass) is ideal for use at Christmas when sprinkled with glue and glitter. Grasses should be hung upside down in bunches to dry.

Step 1—Fill the container with wet Oasis and insert the grasses, the Ivy and six daisies.

Step 2—Add the wide open flowers down the centre, the lower ones tilted forward.

Step 3 (opposite)—Fill in with pink and mauve scabious, and place the largest *Asters* in the centre. Make sure the lower flowers are inserted so that they appear to flow forward over the rim. Fill up with water.

Further decorative grasses which can be grown from seed are *Briza* (Quaking grass), *Setaria italica* (Foxtail millet), *Panicum violaceum* (Millet), *Triticum* (ornamental wheat) and *Bromus* (ornamental oats). *Agrostis* (cloud grass) gives a misty effect.

Step 1

Step 2

Just Two

In Japan the number 'two' is considered to be unlucky, so it is referred to as 'one and one'. Here I show a design of two roses, although any kind of flower can be substituted. Try it with two *Dahlias*, two *Chrysanthemums*, two *Agapanthus* or any round flower, for the more pointed type would not suit this style.

Clive Brooker, the artist potter who made the container, told me he had created the holes in the lower part with no idea as to how they could be utilised. I had the idea of twisting cane in and around the container through the holes. Cane can be obtained from art and craft shops or the Blind Workers Association. It can also be bought in many thicknesses from Dryads Handicrafts Ltd of Northgate, Leicester. Cane, whether twisted, curled or tied in loose knots, will give added flair to any design using a few flowers.

Step 1—Insert a pinholder in the top of the container. Add two roses slightly slanting to the left, placed one below the other close together.

Step 2—Start with a two yard length of cane and insert one end on the pinholder just below the roses. Allow it to spread out to the right, bringing it forward and up, around and behind the shorter flower.

Step 3 (opposite)—Continue swirling the cane up and around the container, finishing by inserting the top end into the pinholder near the start.

NB Cane should be soaked in warm water before using. This makes it more pliable and easy to bend into any shape. Twigs or *Wisteria* tendrils can be substituted.

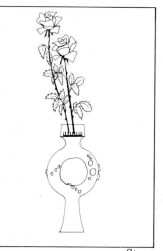

Step 1

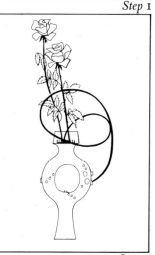

Step 2

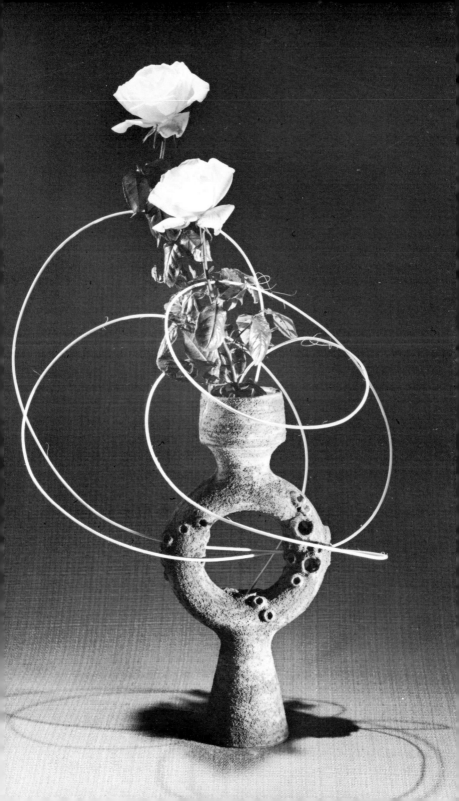

Dignity of Lilies

Often just one rose, a sprig of heather, a branch of foliage, or perhaps one stem of lilies is all that is necessary to make an effective decoration. There is no need to understand dynamic symmetry or spatial influences in these simple designs – but there always should be found a certain studied carelessness. The result is to be gazed upon, not analysed.

Here in a tall pottery container, the lily *longiflorum* (Easter lily) is combined with an interesting piece of root wood and some twigs of Ivy. The wood is optional. I liked its texture, but when I removed it, the lilies appeared to me even more dignified.

Purists might say that the top branch should swerve out more to the right. I agree – that is where it started. But in order to fit it within the measurements of the page, the photographer pushed it upright when I wasn't looking. It was too late to alter it when I saw the result. I can only hope all of you reading this book are not purists.

Step 1—Fill the vase with water, and tuck in the piece of wood. Add the curved branch of Ivy spreading out to the right and curving over to the left.

Step 2—Add two stems of lilies, resting the stem ends on the inside of the container. I removed some of the flower heads to avoid a cluster.

Step 3 (opposite)—Add another swerving branch of Ivy stretching out to the lower right, with a short piece tucked in the wood and hanging over the rim.

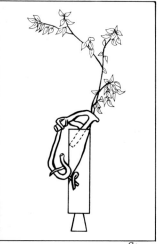

Step 1

Step 2

Red for Gaiety

This mass of varying red flowers and berries is suitable for a gay sideboard or hall decoration. Placed at the end of an oak refectory table with jugs and glasses added, it would also be ideal for an early autumn party.

Designed in a pewter dish which is hardly visible, the arrangement is placed on two straw mats that support the fruit spilling out at the back and side. It can easily be made with red *Gladioli* and red carnations only, interspersed with leaves. But I happened to be in the country at the time so I added some *Antirrhinums*, pink feathery *Astilbe*, two varieties of *Alliums*, and some early Rowan and *Hypericum* (St John's wort) berries.

Step 1

Step 1—Fill the bowl with crumpled wire netting or wet Oasis over a pinholder. Insert the tall *Gladioli*, placing the red carnations at the lower right for width.

Step 2—Add green *Bergenia* leaves leaning backwards, and maroon *Rhus* at the lower left. Place the *Antirrhinums* following the outline, and the crimson *Godetia* in the centre. With a heavy hairpin fix bunches of grapes on to the wire or Oasis.

Step 3 (opposite)—Fill in with pale green *Euphorbia* and pink *Astilbes*. Place the rowan berries recessed, adding cerise and pink *Allium* flowers as an extra effect.

Step 2

Decorative *Alliums* can be planted in November. The cerise one I have used here is *Allium sphaerocephalum*. This is only one of a large family, the biggest variety of which is the *Allium giganteum*, which I often use dried and combined with root wood in modern designs.

Autumn Scene

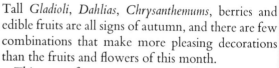

Tall *Gladioli*, *Dahlias*, *Chrysanthemums*, berries and edible fruits are all signs of autumn, and there are few combinations that make more pleasing decorations than the fruits and flowers of this month.

This type of arrangement is suitable for a country house or buffet party decoration. Whether you pick or buy the flowers it is better to recut the stem ends and stand them in deep water for some time before arranging them. There are of course many varieties of *Dahlias* and *Chrysanthemums*, from the large specimen blooms grown for shows to the Pompon and fine spray varieties so much more easy to handle for decorative work. Remove the lower leaves from both these two types of flowers and stand in deep water overnight before using.

Step 1

Step 1—Place a pinholder in the base of a shallow bowl and press a block of wet Oasis on top. Stand the bowl in the centre of a wooden tray. Insert three stems of yellow *Gladioli*, followed by shorter sprays of berries, leaves and *Clematis vitalba* (Old Man's Beard), in the pattern of a triangle.

Step 2—Add large leaves to the lower centre. Follow with *Dahlias*, starting high in the centre and spreading them out low at the sides.

Step 3 (opposite)—Insert maroon-coloured *Chrysanthemums* in the centre with sprays of yellow berries protruding to give a third dimensional effect. Fill the tray with corn cobs, fruits, aubergines and grapes.

Step 2

Dahlia Delight

Few flowers spell early autumn more clearly than colourful *Dahlias*, although the design shown could have been made equally well with *Chrysanthemums* or any other autumn flower.

Dahlias were first introduced in Britain by Lord Bute in 1789. Originally from Mexico, they were named to commemorate Andrea Dahl, a Swedish botanist who was a pupil of Linnaeus, the father of modern botany.

There are many varieties, ranging from the small Pompon decoratives, anemone centred, fringed, and quilled to, among others, the cactus and bizarre varieties, all classified by the National Dahlia Society. For decorative work I do not like the large *Dahlias* but prefer working with the cactus, quilled and small decoratives. However, in the garden they are all striking, especially alongside newly introduced colours.

Here in a wide-topped china container, bronze, flame and yellow *Dahlias* are combined with tassels of *Amaranthus caudatus 'Viridis'* (green love-lies-bleeding) and maroon-coloured *Atriplex hortensis* (mountain spinach). Both of these plants can be grown from seed sown in April or May.

Step 1—Place a pinholder in the bottom of the vase. Cover it with crumpled wire netting, or a block of wet Oasis, which should reach above the rim. Establish the framework of the design by placing the maroon *Atriplex* and grasses in the centre and *Sedum spurium coccineum* low at the sides.

Step 2—Place four *Dahlias* down the centre at different levels and one each side, slightly more forward. Make sure the lowest flower protrudes well over the rim.

Step 3 (opposite)—Fill in from sides to centre with more *Dahlias*, adding stems of love-lies-bleeding high enough to allow the tassels to hang down. Add leaves at the back and fill the vase with water.

Step 1

Step 2

Permanent Beauty

An arrangement of preserved leaves and other plant material can be effective in late autumn and winter decorations. Colour can be introduced by using dried *Larkspur*, *Delphiniums*, *Statice*, borax-dried *Zinnias* and other flowers, but this is a matter of choice. I prefer the brown and beige of glycerined leaves, cones, nuts and artichokes rather than the faded blues and pinks of past summer.

Here in a tall pottery container is a grouping of glycerined *Eucalyptus*, loquat and *Magnolia* leaves, with sprays of beige butcher's broom. The centre is emphasised by gilded dry artichokes and cones.

The skeletonised *Magnolia* leaves and bulrushes can be purchased from the florist. However, you can preserve the other leaves in August by standing the stems in a solution of one part glycerine and two parts hot water for three weeks. The artichokes will dry naturally; spray them with gold paint if desired. The seed sprays on the table are oleander.

Step 1—Place a block of wet Oasis over a pinholder in the top of the container. Make the triangular outline by inserting the bulrushes and foxglove seed stem for height, with the *Eucalyptus* and *Ruscus aculeatus* (butcher's broom) for width.

Step 2—Insert the cones and gilded artichokes backed with brown leaves to give central interest.

Step 3 (opposite)—Add more leaves low over the rim in the front and at the back to avoid a flat effect. Finish by inserting cream skeletonised *Magnolia* leaves to lighten the scheme. These leaves will need a false stem of wire, or a fine hairpin twisted round the base of the leaf will do.

Step 1

Step 2

Tall and Elegant

Not everyone has the space for a large display of flowers in the house, so if this is the problem try a pyramid or cone of flowers. Placed in the centre of a table, on a side table, or made smaller and stood on individual tables for a party, such a display nearly always draws comment.

The variations on this theme are endless. They can be carried out in any colour with almost any round flowers and combined with fruit or berries for extra effect.

Soak an oblong block of Oasis in water for half an hour. Then with a knife slice off the corners at one end to form a cone – do not cut to too fine a point.

Step 1—Stand the Oasis on a heavy pinholder to keep it from toppling over and place this in the base of the container. Insert some buds at the top to establish height and cover the Oasis here and there with short variegated leaves, adding some around the base.

Step 2—Insert short stems of spray *Chrysanthemums* here and there, not too regimented, starting with the bigger blooms at the base.

Step 3 (opposite)—Cover the Oasis with more flower heads and leaves if needed. Finish with short stems of white *Veronica longifolia* or grasses, and trails of Ivy to lighten the effect. Spray or add water daily.

It is not too early to gather interesting seed heads for Winter decorations. A trip in the country will yield untold treasure.

Step 1

Step 2

Pot et Fleur

There is probably no better decoration in autumn and winter than a living plant arrangement. The variations on this theme are endless, though it is preferable to group the type of plants that live happily together and require similar attention.

Despite the attractiveness of living plants, which are even more effective when placed under a lamp, the grouping can be enlivened by the addition of a few cut flowers. These are placed in test tubes of water tucked in between the plants, which are all in their separate pots, or the cut flower stems are inserted into a piece of wet Oasis wedged in between the pots. The French call this type of decoration Pot et Fleur.

Here I use *Cissus antarctica* (kangaroo vine) for height, with trailing Ivy at the left and a maidenhair fern plant swerving out over the rim at the right. In the centre is a small variegated *Peperomia magnoliae-folia* inserted for a change of colour and form.

Step 1—Pack the plant pot container with wet newspaper or moss to prevent the pots from falling to the bottom, and stand the tallest plant in its pot on this false platform.

Step 2—Add the maidenhair or any other swerving plant, tilting the pot so that it leans over the rim at the right. If there is room for another pot, add the Ivy on the left; if not, remove it from the pot wrapping the roots and some damp soil in a small plastic bag. This does not take up so much room and later the Ivy can always be returned to a pot if needed.

Step 3 (opposite)—Tuck in the small *Peperomia* and cover the surface with moss, adding four stems of clear pink *Nerines*. *Nerines* are flowering bulbs which bloom in autumn in a cool greenhouse if the bulbs are planted in July or August. *Nerines Bowdenii* will flourish in the garden if planted in a sheltered sunny spot.

Step 1

Step 2

Space Value

You do not always need a mass of flowers to make a distinctive looking arrangement. Often a few flowers can be given greater importance by the use of tall twigs, bare branches, bleached stripped Ivy, or, as in this case, cane (as used by the chairmakers). It is used here to give height to this modern design of pink *Nerines* and Ivy flowers placed in a Phyllis Sherwood pottery container.

The *Nerine*, a lovely autumn flowering bloom, is named after the Nereids, daughters of a sea god of Greek mythology. It is a South African bulbous plant often grown in cool greenhouses, but many are hardy and will grow outside happily in a well drained spot: for example, at the base of a sunny wall. Plant it in July or August.

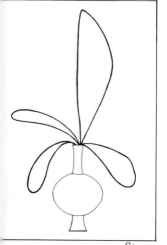

Step 1

Step 1—Using a heavy grade cane, twist four pieces of different lengths, joining the two ends together with wire or a hairpin. Insert the tallest piece upright in the container, followed by another swerving out and downwards at the left. Insert the other two as illustrated. They will not need support in the narrow opening of the vase.

Step 2—Add stems of Ivy leaves and berries as these will act as a background for the flowers. Any other foliage can be substituted.

Step 3 (opposite)—Add the two pink *Nerines*, one pointing down and forward, the other more upright near the rim.

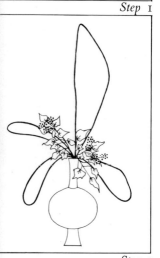

Step 2

As the *Nerines* fade, they can be replaced by other flowers.

Colour Bright

Dark days and dim lights can be relieved by bright coloured flowers. Not everyone's choice, but ideal in many modern settings, carnations and spray *Chrysanthemums* bought from the florist are both long lasting flowers and an added attraction at this time of the year.

Step 1—Fill the green glass vase with water. Insert a long narrow block of wet Oasis, allowing it to reach above the rim. (Alternatively you can use a wide oil funnel placed in the neck of the vase.) Insert the *Montbretia* and a carnation for height, followed by three carnations at the lower right to establish a swerve. Make a cross line with shorter *Montbretia* and flowers.

Step 2—Add the rest of the flame coloured carnations, cutting the stems shorter.

Step 3 (opposite)—Insert stems of rowan or other berries, and add the shorter *Chrysanthemums* clustered around the centre. Further flowers are also placed at the back.

Plant tulips now. I love the early flowering double varieties for massed table designs and the later flowering paeony types such as 'Mount Tacoma' (white) and 'Eros' (rose pink) for pedestals. Few flower arrangers can resist the striped Rembrandt tulips; one called Calypso has broad stripes and streaks of white on a bright cerise background, very effective with early spring foliage.

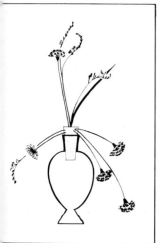

Step 1

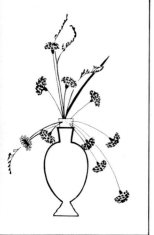

Step 2

Buffet Design

Whether you need a large or small display – one for a party or one just to give colour to your room – *Chrysanthemums* are among the flowers which give the best value. They are probably the longest lasting flowers often giving pleasure for as long as four weeks. Although they are not among my favourite flowers, I must confess I enjoy using the American spray, the rayonnantes (thread-petalled) and the medium flower *Chrysanthemums* especially in the subtle shades of champagne, buff and pink. Recently, Woolmans of Birmingham have introduced a fine pale green one called 'Green Nightingale'.

This arrangement, suitable for a buffet sideboard, groups medium flowered *Chrysanthemums* with pale green grapes and green Ivy.

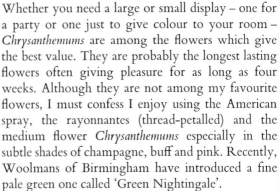

Step 1

Step 1—Press a block of wet Oasis on a large pin-holder and stand it in the bowl-shaped top of this container. Secure the bunches of grapes with the aid of a hairpin bend of wire or a thick hairpin, allowing some of the fruit to flow down and forward, the rest to the sides and back (I used plastic grapes).

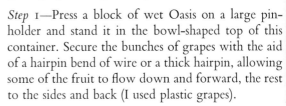

Step 2—Insert stems of Ivy casually, so that the better part of the Oasis is covered.

Step 3 (opposite)—Add the short stems of *Chrysanthemums* all over the back and front, so that no two heads stand level with the other.

Step 2

Winter Delicacy

A bunch of *Freesias* and four stems of spray *Chrysan-themums*, together with some garden or pot plant leaves, are all that are needed to make this delicate arrangement. It can be copied in any other colour at any time of the year using any kind of flower as long as you follow the principle of keeping the finest flowers on the outside and the bigger, rounder or more dominant blooms in the centre.

Keeping this in mind when you visit your florist, you can nearly always visualise a scheme. Take your time when choosing flowers and make friends with your florist. He can nearly always give a helpful suggestion provided he knows you are interested in flowers for decoration rather than 'flowers to put in water'.

Step 1

Step 1—Place a small block of wet Oasis (soak for half an hour) on a pinholder and stand this in the top of the container. Allow the Oasis to reach above the rim. Insert a stem of *Chrysanthemums* in the centre (not too high) and the *Freesias* at the sides.

Step 2—Add more *Chrysanthemums* closer to the rim and further stems at each side of the top centre one.

Step 3 (opposite)—Add leaves around the centre; I used *Arum italicum* which are in the gardens in winter, although large ivy leaves can be substituted. Add some sprays of *Pelargonium crispum* Variegatum as well as trails of Ivy at the sides. Add water to the Oasis each day.

Step 2

With a Difference

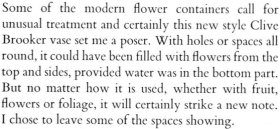

Some of the modern flower containers call for unusual treatment and certainly this new style Clive Brooker vase set me a poser. With holes or spaces all round, it could have been filled with flowers from the top and sides, provided water was in the bottom part. But no matter how it is used, whether with fruit, flowers or foliage, it will certainly strike a new note. I chose to leave some of the spaces showing.

The twists of wood are Ivy branches sprayed with black paint. The rest of the plant material is *Berberis* berries, Ivy berries, and three yellow rayonnantes *Chrysanthemums*.

Step 1—Insert the twists of wood in the top opening, resting the ends against the inside of the container.

Step 2—Place a pinholder in the base and insert the berries and Ivy sprays down through the opening on to the holder.

Step 3 (opposite)—After adding water in the base of the vase, insert three *Chrysanthemums*, one upwards, one forwards, the other one 'in'. Stones or short leaves cover the holder.

Now is the time to buy paint and glitter for your Christmas decorations. Spray grasses with Aerosol glue and shake them in a bag of diamante glitter. Paint the top of poppy seed heads and the edges of ivy leaves with glue, and add glitter to these parts only. For extra effect glue and glitter some candles for your parties.

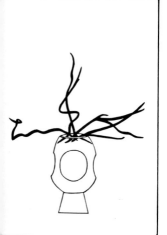

Step 1

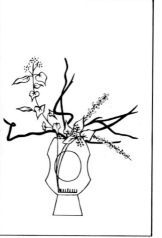

Step 2

Christmas

I have made hundreds of different Christmas decorations over the past years and it was difficult to think of a style which I had not previously designed.

This 'tree', made of variegated holly and berries, was fairly easy to make. Tied up with red velvet ribbon, it looked ideal when finally placed in the centre of my hall table.

It can of course be copied with yew or pine, but whatever greenery you use cut a good number of short stems and use false berries if no others are available. False holly berries can be obtained in the chain stores. Small bunches of them should be wired with a fine hairpin for easy insertion among the leaves.

Soak a block of Oasis for half an hour in water, then trim one end to form a cone. Press this on a pin-holder and stand it in the top of a container. If your container is deep, fill it almost to the top with sand or wet newspaper and stand the cone on this false platform.

Step 1—Insert a ring of foliage around the base and an upright spray for height.

Step 2—Add more short stems in rings starting at the base, continuing until the top is reached.

Step 3 (opposite)—Insert the bunches of false holly berries and with a pin fix the ribbon end at the lower right, winding it around the tree until it reaches to the top. If gold or any other colour is to be your motif for Christmas decorations, spray the 'tree' with gold paint before inserting the berrries and fixing the ribbon.

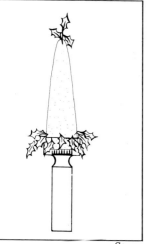

Step 1

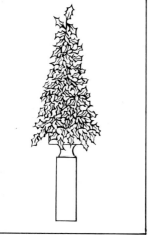

Step 2

Wintry Scene

There are as many ways of decorating at Christmas time as there are different green plants, ribbons, baubles, paints and other accessories. Christmas 'scenes' made with robins, sledges and snowmen always interest the children, while those with a religious motif tend to remind us of the real meaning of the celebration.

All greenery such as yew, pine, cedar, *Cupressus*, should be recut and stood in deep water overnight before used. Then it helps to swish the branches through a solution of Polyfix and water. This is a kind of colourless glue which helps seal the pores and joints, especially of holly, and prevents the leaves from dropping.

Here is a simple but effective design made on a wooden base, a bare branch giving the necessary height.

Step 1—Place a pinholder in a tin of water (or press Oasis on it). Standing this at the left of the base, add the single tall branch. If you prefer, first spray the branch with aerosol false snow. Add another twig leaning out to the left and another shorter one at the lower right.

Step 2—Insert sprays of yew and berried holly, with a climbing stem of Ivy and pieces of pine at the lower left. Cover the holder with a bare piece of wood.

Step 3 (opposite)—Add more wood at the left and back and spray lightly with 'snow'. Finish by including some pine cones and 'robins' to create the scene. This design can be copied using alder catkin branches for height, and Christmas roses (*Helleborus niger*) backed with leaves low down.

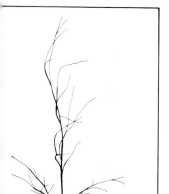

Step 1

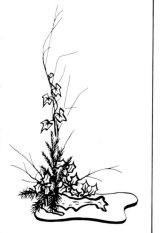

Step 2

Table Centre

Red flowers, green leaves and fruit are ideal for a table centrepiece in December. This arrangement was made 'all round' – that is, the same back and front – so it would be ideal for the centre of a dining table, a buffet table, a sofa table or the hall. The main flowers are from the florist; the *Hydrangeas*, holly and a few late roses come from the garden. The fruit adds to the atmosphere needed when entertaining.

Step 1—Place a block of wet Oasis in a small bowl on a silver tray. Insert three long red carnations low at each side and four Baccara roses in the centre. Next add a bunch or two of pale green grapes, laying them right across the top of the Oasis and fixing the stems down firmly with a heavy hairpin. Repeat the grapes at the back.

Step 2—Add variegated holly or other evergreens in between the carnations. Insert more roses and carnations, some protruding forward and some placed through the grapes. Repeat this at the back.

Step 3 (opposite)—Add leaves of striped *Chlorophytum* at the centre back and insert *Hydrangeas* here and there to give depth and to hide the Oasis. Allow the Ivy to trail down and fix a few apples on sticks as highlights, both front and back.

Seed catalogues are now a joy to pour over. Choose carefully the flowers and plants you will need to carry out your chosen colour schemes. Do not forget to add some unusual items to make your arrangements just a little different.

Step 1

Step 2

Equipment

No-one can paint without brushes or cook without the essential utensils. So it is with flower arranging; if you wish to be proficient you will need a few tools.

You can start quite simply with a pinholder and a dish or a vase and some wire netting, but I show on the opposite page some of the items which will prove of value.

On the top row is a formal vase filled with crumpled wire netting and a metal cone fixed to a stick. The latter is useful for gaining added height when making large church or party arrangements. Often three cones are used. Next is a tall Whitefriars glass vase, useful for a modern design using a few flowers and a branch or cane. The small white vase is ideal for posy arrangements on small tables.

On the next row you see coloured straw mats, which give colour accent when placed under a vase, and a shell filled with a slice of Oasis to hold stems in place. In front are various sizes of pinholder, including one to hold a candle. The white shallow dish is for making modern designs similar to the *Iris* one shown in the month of March. The reel of wire is helpful for tying crumpled wire netting to a large vase – also for tying thin stems together. The apple is pierced with a stick, necessary for giving height to fruit as in the Christmas design. Behind this is a block of Oasis and a black painted base for use with a pinholder and dish for modern designs. At the front is a blue velvet gold-fringed base and a cylinder of Oasis as used in the tin in the basket. Plasticine or permanent adhesive clay is helpful and florists' stub wires are needed for wiring cones and giving false stems to dry plant material. The Wilkinsons flower cutters are a must in my opinion.

Even if you start with only a few of these items, you will avoid frustration which might prevent you from enjoying this expressive art of flower arranging.